The Seminoles of Florida

Culture, Customs, and Conflict

Wendy Conklin, M.A.

Consultants

Dorothy Levin, M.S.ED., MBA
St. Lucie County Schools

Vanessa Ann Gunther, Ph.D.
Department of History
Chapman University

Cassandra Slone
Pinellas County Public Schools

Publishing Credits

Rachelle Cracchiolo, M.S.Ed., *Publisher*
Conni Medina, M.A.Ed., *Managing Editor*
Emily R. Smith, M.A.Ed., *Series Developer*
Diana Kenney, M.A.Ed., NBCT, *Content Director*
Courtney Patterson, *Multimedia Designer*

Image Credits: Cover, pp.1, 4 (front) Tallandier/Bridgeman Images; cover, pp.1, 4, 5, 7, 11, 13 North Wind Picture Archives; pp. 6, 7, 13, 14, 15, 18, 19, 23, 31, 32 State Archives of Florida; p. 9 Marilyn Angel Wynn/Getty Images; p.10 Smithsonian Libraries/Internet Archive; p. 11 (top) Nancy Carter/North Wind Picture Archives, (bottom) CORBIS; pp.12, 13 LOC [LC-DIG-ppmsca-19924]; p. 15 LOC [g3930.ct000731]; p. 16 (background) Creative Commons File:Dade-battlefield-bushnell hill pano02.jpg by Ebyabe used under CC BY-SA 3.0, (bottom) Creative Commons File:Dade-battlefield-bushnell plaque02.jpg by Ebyabe used under CC BY-SA 3.0, (top) Records of the United States Senate, 1789–1990; Record Group 46; Records of the United States Senate, 1789–1990; National Archives; p.17 AAA Photostock/Alamy; p.19 Kenneth Riley/National Geographic/Getty Images; p.20 Saint Louis Art Museum; p. 22 Wikimedia Commons/Public Domain; pp. 24–25 NARA [306073-A]; p. 25 From the Albert Johannsen Collection at Northern Illinois University; pp. 26, 29 Historic Florida/Alamy; pp. 26–27, 29 M&N/Alamy; p.27 Ruth Peterkin/Shutterstock.com; p.29 Marilyn Angel Wynn/Getty Images; all other images from iStock and/or Shutterstock.

Library of Congress Cataloging-in-Publication Data

Names: Conklin, Wendy, author.
Title: The Seminoles of Florida : culture, customs, and conflict / Wendy
 Conklin, M.A.
Description: Huntington Beach, CA : Teacher Created Materials, 2017. |
 Includes index.
Identifiers: LCCN 2016014349 (print) | LCCN 2016015179 (ebook) | ISBN
 9781493835355 (pbk.) | ISBN 9781433388026 (eBook)
Subjects: LCSH: Seminole Indians--History--Juvenile literature. | Seminole
 Indians--Social life and customs--Juvenile literature.
Classification: LCC E99.S28 C725 2017 (print) | LCC E99.S28 (ebook) | DDC
 975.9004/973859--dc23
LC record available at https://lccn.loc.gov/2016014349

Teacher Created Materials
5301 Oceanus Drive
Huntington Beach, CA 92649-1030
http://www.tcmpub.com

ISBN 978-1-4938-3535-5

Table of Contents

A New Tribe

"The agent tells us we must go away from the lands we live on—our homes, and the graves of our Fathers….When the agent tells me to go from my home, I hate him, because I love my home, and will not go from it." These are the words of the young Seminole leader, Osceola. What caused this leader to say such strong words? To answer this question, let's start at the beginning.

In the 1700s, some American Indian tribes from Georgia and Alabama moved south. Explorers from Europe had moved into their lands. Contact with these white **settlers** was not friendly. The tribes found themselves at odds with other tribes, too. They wanted to find a place where they could live in peace. They moved to what we now know as Florida. They merged with other tribes that were there. By the 1700s, this new group became known as the *Seminoles.* Translated, the name means "runaways."

Osceola

Seminoles prepare to fight.

Culture and Daily Life

When Seminoles first moved to northern Florida, they built towns. Each town had 16 to 60 structures. These houses were grouped by twos and were a lot like log cabins. One house was larger than the other. It had two to three rooms for cooking, eating, and sleeping. The other was used to store food and supplies. Each pair of houses had a garden where people grew **maize**, beans, and melons. There were also larger farms in the towns. Women tended these fields of crops where the town grew things, such as taro and rice.

Farming wasn't their only source of food. Young boys often fished, while older men hunted bears and deer. They herded cattle with the help of horses and dogs. They also carved canoes. These canoes helped them to explore the land around Florida. They explored the southern part of Florida known as the **Everglades**. They traveled to the Bahamas and Cuba to trade for coffee and sugar.

Koonti

Seminole Indians used a strainer like the one shown here to make Koonti flour. Koonti is a starchy root. The koonti is mashed into a pulp. Then it is washed, strained, and dried to make the flour.

Once a year, the Seminoles gathered from nearby towns. They held the Green Corn Ceremony. It was an event to give thanks and to mark the change in seasons. They gave thanks for the food they had grown. They held rituals that marked children entering adulthood. They forgave each other and settled disputes. All crimes except murder could be addressed and forgiven.

Dancing was also an important part of the festival. One dance was the Stomp Dance. Dancers stomped and shuffled for hours. This dance often started the festivities. It got everyone involved. Male and female dancers moved in rhythm to create a swirling wind of energy that carried everyone into a new year.

A Symbol of Life

The Seminoles saw ripened corn as a symbol of life. Corn starts from seeds and grows and matures over time. The life cycle of the corn mirrored that of the people, while also sustaining their lives.

Seminoles perform the Stomp Dance.

First Seminole War

Florida changed hands many times over the years. When the Seminoles first moved to the area, it was controlled by Spain. Rule switched to the British in 1763. Then, it went back to Spain in 1783.

At the same time, the United States was expanding. The new country was using more slave labor. African slaves formed the bulk of this labor force. Although Florida had slaves, Spain's policies gave slaves more rights. As a result, many slaves from the United States tried to escape to Florida. The Spanish in Florida were happy to have more people join their ranks. Their workforce grew. They had more troops.

The Seminoles gave runaway slaves a safe place to live. The slaves who joined the tribe came to be known as Black Seminoles. They were still slaves, but they were treated better. Some even married Seminoles.

a Black Seminole

Flags from Great Britain, Spain, and the United States fly in St. Augustine as a symbol of history.

Slaves work in Spanish-ruled Florida.

This is an 1837 depiction of the Seminoles attacking a fort in 1835.

There was already tension between the United States and the Seminoles. The British gave the tribe weapons during the War of 1812. The tribe helped the British in their fight against the Americans. The United States was not pleased with the tribe's actions. And giving **refuge** to escaped slaves made matters worse.

In November 1817, tensions reached an all-time high. Edmund Gaines, the commander at Fort Scott, accused some Seminoles of murdering white settlers. He asked the **chief**, Neamathla, to turn in the men. He refused. Under the command of General Andrew Jackson, Gaines sent in soldiers. The soldiers killed about 20 men. They chased the other people from the town into the swamps. They burned the town to the ground.

General Andrew Jackson addresses his troops in the First Seminole War.

Battles continued back and forth for two months. One group would attack the other. Then, a counterattack would swiftly follow. Plantations were destroyed. Towns were leveled. Jackson's troops destroyed Seminole towns. They attacked Spanish forts. In the end, Spain saw that it had lost control over Florida. The fighting stopped in 1818. Spain gave Florida to the United States in 1819 per the terms of the Adams-Onís **treaty**.

U.S. soldiers capture Seminole chiefs.

After the War

In 1821, Florida became a U.S. **territory**. For the time being, the Seminoles kept living on their land. But conflicts between the tribe and white settlers did not end. In 1822, a man named William Duval governed Florida. The settlers wrote him letters about the Seminoles. They charged the tribe with stealing cattle and slaves. He felt pressured to act. So in 1823, he asked the tribe's leaders to sign a treaty. It was called the Treaty of Moultrie Creek.

The treaty stated that the tribe would give up all rights to its land in Florida. The tribe would move to a **reservation** in Central Florida. The people would abide by the laws of the United States. They would not provide shelter to escaped slaves. The tribe's trade with the Bahamas and Cuba would be restricted. In return, the U.S. government would protect the tribe. The tribe would receive corn, meat, and salt for 12 months to make up for the crops they would have to leave behind. The people would also get tools, goods, and a monthly payment from the government. The tribe signed the treaty and moved.

William Duval

A Reward for Loyalty

An article was later added to the Treaty of Moultrie Creek. It stated that six chiefs, who they called the Apalachicola (ap-uh-lach-ih-KOH-luh) band of Creek Indians, could stay on their land. They would not have to move to the reservation. This group had helped the United States during the First Seminole War. This was a reward for their loyalty.

This historical marker stands where the Treaty of Moultrie Creek was signed.

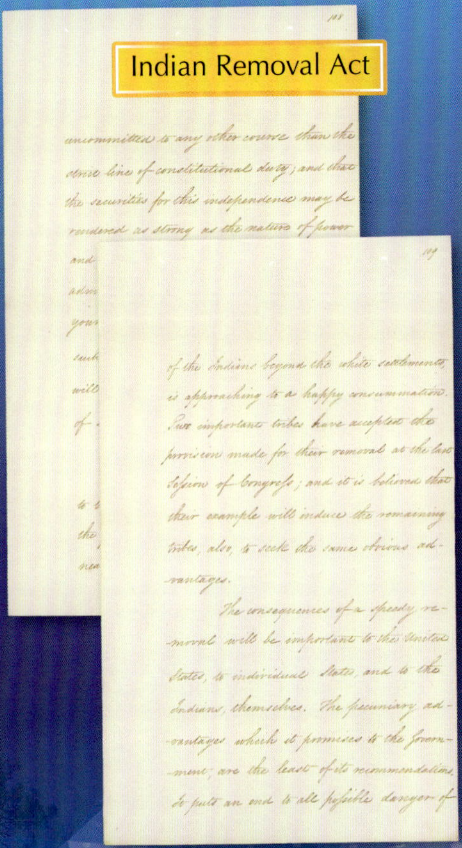
108

uncommitted to any other course than the strict line of constitutional duty; and that the securities for this independence may be rendered as strong as the nature of power

109

of the Indians beyond the white settlements is approaching to a happy consummation. Two important tribes have accepted the provision made for their removal at the last session of Congress; and it is believed that their example will induce the remaining tribes, also, to seek the same obvious advantages.

The consequences of a speedy removal will be important to the United States, to individual States, and to the Indians, themselves. The pecuniary advantages which it promises to the Government, are the least of its recommendations. It puts an end to all possible danger of

Indian Removal Act

The Seminoles did not want to stay on the new land. The boundaries of the land kept changing. A drought made the land poor for farming. The settlers weren't content, either. They wanted the tribe removed from the whole territory.

In 1829, Andrew Jackson became president. In 1830, he signed the **Indian Removal Act**. The act stated that all American Indian tribes would have to move west of the Mississippi River. Each tribe would receive its own land. The Seminoles signed the Treaty of Payne's Landing. It let a group of their leaders travel west to assess the land.

Dade's Battlefield today

Once there, they were persuaded to move. They signed the Treaty of Fort Gibson. It set 1835 as the date for **emigration**. When they got back to Florida, they said they had been tricked into signing the treaty.

In late 1835, the Seminoles refused to move. They began a string of attacks. One of those was Dade's Battle. The Americans called it the Dade Massacre. Only one white soldier who had fought the whole battle survived long enough to recount the fight. On the same day, a Seminole named Osceola killed Indian Agent Wiley Thompson. Osceola instantly became a wanted man. The Second Seminole War had begun.

Billy Powell (Osceola)

A Different Name

Billy Powell was born in 1804 in a Creek village in Alabama. Most people know him as Osceola. His name was changed when he and his mother moved from Alabama to Florida to join the Seminoles.

A Second War Is Waged

The Second Seminole War proved to be the longest of the three wars. It was also the most costly. Osceola led the Seminole warriors in defense of their land. They were skilled fighters. They were able to hide in the depths of the swamps and forests. The U.S. Army was not used to this **guerrilla warfare**.

In 1836, General Thomas Jesup took command. He planned carefully. He built new forts. In 1837, Seminole leaders signed a cease-fire with Jesup. They said they would move west. Jesup was sure he had won. Instead, the Seminoles used the cease-fire time to get more supplies and firearms.

General Thomas Jesup

Florida swamp

Over Budget

The United States spent over $30 million fighting the Seminoles. At the time, the total federal budget was only about $25 million.

A soldier arrests Osceola.

That same year, Osceola and another leader named Coacoochee, or Wild Cat, met with U.S. troops. They went to discuss peace. But they had been tricked. Despite the **truce**, Jesup ordered Osceola to be captured. The rules of war had been broken. Osceola's fame grew.

The soldiers took Osceola and Wild Cat to Fort Marion. There, Wild Cat refused to eat. Soon, he lost enough weight. He squeezed through the bars and escaped. But, Osceola was sick. He stayed in prison as Wild Cat led the Seminoles. A year later, soldiers moved him to another fort. He died in 1838 while in prison there.

Wild Cat escapes from jail.

Seminole leaders such as Wild Cat and Holata Micco, or Billy Bowlegs, kept up the fight for a few more years. Some of the Seminoles gave up. They moved west. Many hid in the Everglades where soldiers could not find them. Jesup kept weakening Seminole lines. He promised freedom to Black Seminoles who moved. Both sides suffered great losses in battle.

Billy Bowlegs leads Seminole warriors through the Everglades.

Billy Bowlegs

Holata Micco's English name was actually Billy Bolek. But white settlers called him Billy Bowlegs, and the name stuck.

In August 1842, Bowlegs surrendered for his people. The United States declared an end to the war. It had lasted for seven years. The United States lost 1,500 soldiers and $30 million. About 4,000 Seminoles went to live in the West. Less than 500 Seminoles stayed in Florida. Some lived in the Everglades. Some lived in Big Cypress Swamp. No treaty was signed, but they were allowed to stay.

Big Cypress Swamp

Third and Final War

After the second war, life for those who stayed in Florida did not get any better. Florida became a state in 1845. More people started to pour in looking for land. White settlers continued to move in on the tribes. It wasn't long before the U.S. Army met with Bowlegs. They asked the tribe, once again, to move west. But Bowlegs didn't give in.

In the fall of 1855, a small force of soldiers marched through Big Cypress Swamp. They cut down trees. They cut down fruit that belonged to Bowlegs. Bowlegs did not want his people harassed any longer. He and his men attacked the nearby military camp. This sparked the Third Seminole War.

Billy Bowlegs

early American settlers in Florida

The war continued for two more years. In that time, the U.S. Army **waged** many small battles. But, the country had learned its lesson. It didn't want to spend the amounts of money it had during the Second Seminole War. So, it spent time seeking out Seminole towns. Troops searched through the swamps. They used boats to search remote swampland. They destroyed towns. Seminoles who were found were often captured and sent west.

Seminoles hide in the swamps.

In 1858, Bowlegs surrendered. The war was over. The government gave him $8,000 to move west. He took 165 of his people with him. When he left, less than 200 Seminoles remained in the Everglades. They refused to leave.

This 1865 book tells a fictional tale about Billy Bowlegs.

Seminoles Today

As the years went by, the health of the Everglades dwindled. More people moved to the state. Some of them drained water from the swamps. They wanted to build, and they needed dry land to do so. But people fought to protect the swamps. Everglades National Park is now protected. The Seminoles play a big part in keeping it healthy.

In 1957, the U.S. government recognized the Seminole Tribe of Florida. The tribe is its own nation. It receives some support from the U.S. government for its people. In return, the tribe will not file any more land claims. A second group from the tribe asked to be recognized in 1962—the Miccosukee (mihk-uh-SOO-kee) Tribe of Indians of Florida. There is also a third group. It is called the Independent Seminoles. Its people are not part of either tribe. They do not want to take the government's deal.

Today, most people from the tribes still live on reservations. They value education. They excel in business. They honor their culture. They teach their children to have the strength of their ancestors.

These students attend a school on a reservation.

Florida State University

Florida State University works with the Seminole Tribe of Florida to ensure that the school's Seminole warrior "Osceola" is a respectful depiction of the legendary hero. The clothing that the mascot wears when he rides out on the football field has been approved by, and is often handmade, by the tribe.

Author It!

Write an acrostic poem that tells about the Seminole Indians. Write *Seminole* down the left side on your paper. For each letter, write a word or phrase that describes Seminole culture or history. Share your poem with a friend or family member.

Glossary

chief—a leader or ruler of a group of people

emigration—to leave a country or region to live elsewhere

Everglades—a vast area of swampy wetlands south of Lake Okeechobee

guerrilla warfare—unexpected attacks against an army carried out by a group of people

Indian Removal Act—a law that relocated American Indians from their homelands to land west of the Mississippi River

maize—American Indian word for corn

refuge—shelter or protection from danger

reservation—land set aside especially for American Indians to live and work

settlers—people who go to a new place to live

territory—an area of land that is controlled by the government

treaty—a formal agreement made between two or more countries or groups

truce—a mutual agreement between enemies to stop fighting for a period of time

waged—started and continued

Index

DADE BATTLEFIELD
HAS BEEN DESIGNATED A
NATIONAL
HISTORIC LANDMARK
THIS SITE POSSESSES NATIONAL SIGNIFICANCE
IN COMMEMORATING THE HISTORY OF THE
UNITED STATES OF AMERICA
1974
NATIONAL PARK SERVICE
UNITED STATES DEPARTMENT OF THE INTERIOR

Your Turn!

Postcard from Fort Marion

This postcard shows Osceola imprisoned at Fort Marion. How does this picture compare to the one of him on page 4 of this book? What is similar about the two portrayals? What is different? Create a Venn diagram to record your observations.